The Secret Weapon of a Master Direct Response Online Copywriter

How to Position your Brand for Success, Based on the Research of Swiss Psychiatrist Carl Jung

by Peter A. Schaible

ISBN 0-9746962-2-6

For Barbara

Contents

Contents

Introduction: The four fundamental questions you must ask and answer

Years ago, bestselling author and small business expert Michael Gerber got me accustomed to asking my clients four fundamental questions about their businesses. You might be amazed by how few people can answer all four questions with any degree of confidence.

The questions are:

1. What business are you in?

2. Who is your customer?

3. Why does he or she buy your products or services?

4. How do you know this? (What is the evidence or proof?)

The answer to question number one - *What business are you in?* - may seem obvious, but generally it's not.

If you have an automobile service and repair garage, you may think that you're in the business of doing oil changes, tune-ups and engine repairs. But depending on how you position your service in the customer's mind, you may be in an entirely different business.

If you're a Jiffy Lube franchisee, you're in the business of providing your customers with fast and professional maintenance service for their vehicles. Your customers value speed and economy, and getting a "good deal" is among their highest criteria.

If you're John O'Connor, the owner of Shade Tree Garage in Morristown, New Jersey, that's not the business you're in and that's not your customer. Everybody employed by Shade Tree Garage - service writers, technicians, detailers and porters - knows that Shade Tree Garage is in the business giving its customers peace of mind about the safety and reliability of their cars.

That's a very different mindset than they have at Jiffy Lube, and an entirely different business model.

The answer to question number 2 - *Who is your customer?* - can be found by organizing around your target audience.

Many marketers and direct response copywriters begin a campaign or an assignment by trying to learn everything they can about the product.

Good start, but that's only part of the job.

In order to write effective, persuasive copy, you also want to know everything you can about the kind of person who is most likely to buy your product or service.

Male or female? Age? Profession? Single, married or divorced?

Income? Education? Geographic location?

And that's only the beginning.

Why? Because demographic and psychographic profiles provide priceless information about why people buy - if you learn how to interpret them.

Your goal should be to organize the marketing campaign and sales messages around the customer. And never forget, the customer, first and foremost, is a complex, emotional human being.

The customer is a person, even when you're marketing an industrial commodity to another business. You don't sell to other companies or industries, you sell to other people.

And while demographics and psychographics are very useful, they don't necessarily dictate the target audience of your sales letter. Often, you will want to address your message not to "who they are" but to "who they want to be."

For example, the publisher of a newsletter for landlords knows that 80 percent of his readers own three or less rental properties - most of them one-family homes or duplexes. But most of these landlords aspire to own larger rental properties. So his sales copy addresses apartment house owners.

Publisher Don Nicholas calls this "aspirational" copywriting.

The subscribers to magazines such as *Road and Track,* and *Car and Driver*, are not generally the owners of exotic sports cars. They're the people who aspire to someday owning an exotic sports car. These magazines help them get closer to their dreams.

Or as advertising legend David Ogilvy said, "People buy products that project who they want to be, not who they are."

The Take-Away: The little fish always like to read about the big fish. The big fish seldom care to read about the little fish.

The most fundamental question: Why do they buy?

The answer to question number 3 - *Why do they buy?* - is the most complicated to answer. The reasons people buy are not well known and are frequently misunderstood.

That's because most people don't really know why they make a preferential decision for one product or service over another. They may think they understand their process for making a purchase decision, but it generally happens in the unconscious mind.

Most of us are self-absorbed, walking around in a trance. In fact, when I studied hypnotism years ago, my instructor, John LaValle, made a profound observation about the work of changing another person's state of consciousness.

"The trick is not getting someone into a state of trance," John said, "It's getting him out of the trance he's already in." That makes sense to me.

Every day we are bombarded by media messages. Between TV, radio, newspapers, magazines, signs, the Internet, etc., each of us sees hundreds of advertisements every single day. All are competing for our attention - consciously and unconsciously.

As consumers, we sort all these incoming communications for self-interest. The messages that don't interest us personally and emotionally, don't get a nanosecond of our attention.

This is true of your prospective customer. Most people don't care about your product or service. They only care about what your product or service can do for them. Specifically, the customer cares about your product only as it compliments his self-concept and gratifies his ego.

"Don't tell me about your grass seed," he says, "talk to me about my lawn."

What he really means is (although he doesn't consciously know it), "Don't tell me about your grass seed, appeal to how a beautiful lawn will make me the envy of my neighbors and compliment my self-image as a prosperous, successful person."

The Take-Away: Your potential customer doesn't care about your product. He only cares about his own gratification.

Online copywriting for the unconscious mind

The freelance copywriter's dream is always the same. A comfortable life style. No commute. No irascible bosses.

Getting paid for playing with words. Creating something magical. Influencing behavior.

And, of course, reaping the results: Awards and accolades. The admiration of clients and peers. Financial independence.

Who wouldn't want a job like that? Or as my friend, copywriter John Clausen explains his career choice, "Too lazy to work, too nervous to steal."

But as anyone who has tried to make a good living at this craft knows, it's not as easy as it looks. And even if you've achieved a certain level of success as a print advertising copywriter, the Internet has changed everything. Online marketing requires new skills and forces us to reexamine everything we thought was immutable.

It's not just computer technology that's changed our world, it's also what Dr. Robert Cialdini calls, "the new science of persuasion." Psychologists and neurologists have made startling discoveries that help to explain human behavior - including why people buy - with models that are at once both new and eerily familiar.

Science now tells us we have three brains

Dr. Paul MacLean, Chief of the Laboratory of Brain Evolution and Behavior at the National Institute of Mental

Health, says our brains have evolved through three primary stages. His theory of the Triune Brain proposes that our skull holds not one brain, but three.

First is the reptilian brain - responsible for instinctive, automatic, basic survival behaviors like fight or flight, hunger, fear and reproduction. It's also the center for aggression, courtship, mating, and territorial defense.

Second is the limbic brain, which governs our emotions. It collects sensory information and screens it for emotional relevance.

And last, the neocortex brain - the control center for language and rational thinking. It's the center for reading, speaking, writing and reasoning. It's responsible for awareness, conscious thought and logic.

As a copywriter, you should be interested in all three brains, particularly the connection between the limbic and the reptilian, which Dr. G. Clotaire Rapaille calls, "the logic of emotion" or how the emotions deal with the urges, instincts and needs we all have.

Dr. Rapaille is a child psychiatrist turned marketing researcher who convincingly argues that buying decisions have nothing to do with practical needs or rational decision making.

It's the reptilian brain - the preconscious part where archetypes and primitive associations are imprinted - that makes our purchase decisions. It's reptilian because we share it in common with reptiles like alligators and lizards.

The single focus of the reptilian brain is survival. The reptilian brain doesn't entertain abstract thoughts; it doesn't feel complex emotions such as love, envy and compassion.

You can stimulate the reptilian brain with words, but it operates instinctively and without conscious thought. And so we buy what we want, not necessarily what we need.

Our carefully written stories and product descriptions are capable of pushing the reptilian hot buttons that stimulate the most primitive impulses. Beyond the reptilian, our words push limbic hot buttons - higher level emotions that may be associated with family, children, parents, etc.

As marketers, we need to appeal to all three brains in order to evoke a congruent purchase decision from our prospective customer.

Every human has the same basic (and often unspoken) needs. Everyone wants to be sexier, smarter, wealthier, secure, comfortable, warm, well-fed, etc. Additionally, we have needs that go beyond these basics that we are not even aware of.

Now, I'm not suggesting that everybody is exactly the same. We're all unique. But we are also very much alike. The similarities of our behaviors can be observed, and in many instances, can be predicted.

So, the answer to question number three, "Why does your customer buy?" is never simple. But you can be certain of this. His purchase decisions - indeed everyone's purchase decisions - are never wholly rational, even when buying commodities or making B2B transactions.

Purchase decisions are made in the reptilian part of the human brain. Most of the time, we buy what we want, not necessarily what we need.

But because we need to rationalize these purchases, the copywriter's job is to provide "reasons why," in effect, giving the purchaser the "rational armament" with which to defend his purchase decision.

So all of us who call ourselves marketers are using (or misusing) the power of words to persuade someone else to buy our products.

But here's the distinction that I make. A good salesman gets the customer to buy the product that the buyer truly wants and can afford.

By contrast, a con man will sell you anything, regardless of quality, regardless of whether it's appropriate for you, regardless of whether you can afford it. His goal is to separate you from your money. Nothing else matters to him.

The Take-Away: Your customer buys what he wants, not necessarily what he needs, but justifies his purchase decisions with rationalizations.

Now think about something you recently bought that you are really, really happy with. For me, it's my new glasses. I am so glad that someone talked me into getting the "Transitions" lenses that change color - darkening when you're in the sun and lightening up when you're inside or in the shade. Love 'em! I'll never have another pair of glasses without 'em!

So I got sold Transitions lenses by a great sales person. And I'm very grateful for the sales job that she did. She got me to own a product I really, really like, but wasn't expecting to buy.

Note, too, that there will always be some personal gratification associated with your purchase decision. For instance, I own both a $3,500 Rolex wrist watch that I bought in the Caribbean for $1,800, and a $175 Pulsar wrist watch that I got on sale in a factory outlet store for $27. The Pulsar has more function and keeps better time.

But the Rolex gratifies my ego. It makes a statement about my business success and my ability to provide for myself and my family. And I can afford it. In fact, I bought it nearly 25 years ago to reward myself for my first $1 million year in business!

Where is the evidence?

Question number four - How do you know? - is the hardest to answer because most businesses haven't got the foggiest idea why a consumer prefers and buys their product over that of the competition. They have no evidence procedure; they're just guessing.

Frequently, business managers say they believe that consumers buy their product because it is better than the competition, but that's seldom true. In fact, in many cases, the consumer doesn't know what the better product is. Often, nobody does.

Who makes the best personal computer? IBM? Dell? Hewlett-Packard? How do you know?

Is a Buick intrinsically better than a Ford? Is a John-Deere mower better than a Toro or a Honda?

Consumer Reports magazine may have some objective criteria for testing products, but most of us consumers don't. All we have is a bunch of impressions in our brains, our neighbor's expert opinion - there's always one guy in every neighborhood who's an expert - and our basic instincts about what constitutes the right brand.

Significantly, the average consumer doesn't know why he prefers and chooses to buy one product over another. At least, he doesn't know consciously. The answer lies deep in his psyche.

If you make or market a product, this should be unacceptable to you. If you're in business, you need to know why someone buys your product.

If you're marketing the product and writing the sales promotion copy, you must know (or at least have a darned good idea) why a customer makes a preferential decision for your product over another.

This information is far too important to be left entirely to chance.

For the answer to how we know, we tap into some ancient, universal wisdom.

The Take-Away: If you understand precisely why someone buys, you can position your product or service to be more appealing.

Targeting consumer archetypes

We owe a huge debt to Margaret Mark and Carol Pearson for defining the basic consumer archetypes in their seminal book, The Hero and the Outlaw. All thoughtful marketers do.

The term archetype was advanced by the Swiss psychiatrist Carl Jung in the early 20th century to analyze personality types. Archetypes help explain personality. Variations on the archetype model include the Enneagram and the Myers-Briggs Type Indicator®.

According to Jung, archetypes are characters, images, plot patterns, rituals, and settings that are shared by diverse cultures. Jung believed that archetypes are part of humanity's "collective unconscious" and that they appear in literature, myth, folklore, and rituals from a wide range of cultures.

Don't glaze over now. This is very powerful information. By symbolizing our core human desires, archetypes can evoke deep, strong emotions. Archetypes are emotionally charged images and thought forms that have universal meaning.

Archetypes can provide us with an understanding of the unconscious instincts that affect our motivations and behaviors. They can help us predict how we will respond to common human experiences.

I think of these archetypal patterns as blueprints or DNA that trigger memories from deep within our subconscious.

If you adopt the archetype model for defining and explaining the values and motivations of human beings, you can create products, brands and marketing campaigns with specific appeal to clearly defined, targeted customers.

In this model, there are essentially 12 customer archetypes, and each has specific, distinctive values, goals and fears. And while a single archetype per individual prevails, it is not uncommon that an individual also fits secondary archetypes, resulting in a blended model.

If you understand each of the different archetypes, and the major gratification each seeks, you can discover how to make your product appeal to its most likely archetypal customer.

At the heart of a great sales letter is a story about the product that distinguishes it from all other products. Archetypes help the copywriter create that story and target it to the most receptive potential customers.

The Take-Away: When you understand how a customer gets his major gratifications in life, you'll discover his "hot buttons" for buying.

The Hero Archetype

The Hero archetype is variously known as the warrior, the crusader, the rescuer, the superhero, the solder, the winning athlete, the dragon slayer, the competitor and the team player.

Heroes get their greatest gratification from being perceived as courageous, strong, powerful and competent. The Hero thinks of himself as helping other people by acting courageously.

The Hero sees himself as a protector of the innocent, the weak, and - at the risk of being accused of sexism - women. (Ironically, the Hero's greatest fantasy is sexual promiscuity without consequences.)

The Hero customer is usually ambitious and often seeks out challenges. His greatest fear is weakness, vulnerability and cowardice. At his worst, the Hero is arrogant, combative, ruthless and obsessed with winning.

If you want to invoke anxiety in a Hero customer, your sales promotion copy should exploit his fear of inadequacy, failure or "wimping out."

As Michael Gerber points out, popular magazines illustrate how much American culture reveres the Hero archetype.

- American Legion magazine celebrates the war Hero.

- Fortune magazine celebrates the business Hero.

- Sports Illustrated celebrates the athlete Hero.

- Boy's Life magazine is one of the preferred

publications for Heroes in training. So are numerous comic books.

Other Hero brands

- John Wayne (American actor who epitomized ruggedly individualistic masculinity)

- John Glenn (American astronaut; Marine Corps fighter pilot)

- Susan B. Anthony (American civil rights leader)

- James Bond (fictional British secret agent 007)

- Superman (fictional character; comic book superhero)

- Wonder Woman (fictional character; DC Comics super heroine)

- John F. Kennedy (charismatic U.S. president; senator; war hero; Pulitzer prize-winning author)

- Teddy Roosevelt (U.S. president; governor of New York; historian; naturalist; explorer; author; soldier)

- Dwight Eisenhower (U.S. president; Army general; Supreme Commander of the Allied forces in Europe)

- Martin Luther King (leader of the American civil rights movement; Baptist minister)

- Nelson Mandela (former president of South Africa; anti-apartheid activist)

- Star Wars

- Saving Private Ryan

- United States Marine Corps ("The few. The proud.")

- Nike, ("Just do it!"; the sportswear and equipment supplier takes its name from the Greek goddess of victory)

- FedEx ("The World On Time")

- Old Spice ("The mark of a man.")

- American Red Cross (provides emergency assistance, disaster relief and education)

- most video games

- Marlboro cigarettes (distilled their manly imagery into the rugged cowboys known as the "Marlboro Men.")

- PricewaterhouseCoopers ("Join us. Together we can change the world.")

- L'Oreal ("Wrinkle-free defense cream.")

- Ford trucks ("Built Ford tough.")

Appealing to the Hero Consumer Archetype

The Hero consumer archetype wants to believe in something concrete. He appreciates quality, strength and clarity. He likes to compete and, above all, to win.

Hero brands are all about superior performance. Cars, copiers, cameras - it doesn't matter - your product will appeal to the Hero consumer archetype if it helps him perform at a higher level. Or if it helps him to demonstrate his strength, or to stand for something, or to "make a difference."

Emphasize your product's ability to do a tough job efficiently and well, and it will appeal to the Hero consumer archetype.

Alternatively, have a well-defined opponent or competitor that your product can claim to beat, and you will appeal to the Hero consumer archetype.

The Take-Away: Hero consumers are obsessed with performance. They require products that reinforce their self-image as strong, competent, powerful winners.

The Sage Archetype

The Sage archetype is variously known as the expert, the scholar, the detective, the philosopher, the teacher, the mentor and the wizard.

Sages get their greatest gratification from being perceived as intelligent, knowledgeable and wise. The Sage thinks of himself as helping other people by understanding their world.

The Sage sees himself as a seeker of truth, a skeptic, a critic and an innovative thinker. At his best, the Sage projects wisdom, confidence and mastery. At his worst, the Sage is dogmatic or living in an ivory tower and disconnected from the real world.

If you want to invoke anxiety in a Sage consumer, threaten him with confusion or with not having enough information. Then offer your product as the logical solution to this information deficit.

Be especially careful not to confuse the Sage consumer about your product, how to order it, the price, or any other detail. And never allow the Sage consumer to feel incompetent or pressured. If he is confused, the Sage consumer will always reject your product or service.

Like all consumers, the Sage makes emotional purchase decisions with his reptilian brain, but is often unable to recognize this or unwilling to admit it. Therefore, the Sage consumer needs a rational alibi to justify his purely emotional decisions.

So, the Sage consumer usually wants copious amounts of hard data and is comfortable with all the specifications, metrics and minutia of your product. "The more you tell, the more you sell," is especially true when targeting your product to the Sage consumer.

Sage consumers love products that are based on scientific breakthroughs and esoteric knowledge. They are rabid consumers of books, videos and other information products.

Sage consumers can be early adopters of new technology and products, especially if you differentiate your product from others whose quality or performance is suspicious.

Famous Sages

- Socrates (classical Greek philosopher, martyr)

- Confucius (Chinese thinker and social philosopher)

- The Buddha (spiritual teacher from ancient India and the founder of Buddhism)

- Galileo (Tuscan physicist, mathematician, astronomer, and philosopher)

- Einstein (German-born theoretical physicist)

- George Carlin (standup comedian, actor and author)

- Phyllis Diller (comedienne; pioneer of female stand-up comedy)

- Walter Cronkite (TV journalist and anchorman; "the most trusted man in America"; also a Caregiver)

- Obi Wan Kenobi (fictional character in Star Wars; a Jedi Master, who then tutors Luke Skywalker to use the Force)

- Yoda (fictional character in Star Wars, trains Luke Skywalker in the ways of the Jedi)

- Oprah Winfrey ("The Black Madonna")

- Sherlock Holmes (fictional master detective)

- Al Gore (former U.S. Vice President and intellectual)

- Deepak Chopra (an Indian medical doctor and writer; has written extensively on spirituality)

- Billy Graham (evangelist; number seven on Gallup's list of most admired people for the 20th century)

Sage Brands

- Harvard University (the oldest institution of higher learning in the United States)

- Johns Hopkins University (esteemed for its medical, scientific, and international studies programs)

- McKinsey (the most prestigious firm in the management consulting industry)

- Educational Testing Service (world's largest private educational testing and measurement organization)

- Betty Crocker (fictional cookbook author for American food company General Mills)

- The New York Times (regarded as the national newspaper of record)

- Consumer Reports (American magazine that publishes reviews and comparisons of consumer products. "We test, inform and protect.")

- National Public Radio (voted the most trusted news source in the US)

- The New York Times ("All the news that's fit to print.")

- CNN (major news cable television network)

- Barnes & Noble (specialty book retailer)

- The Discovery Channel (TV channel that provides documentary programming on popular science, technology, and history)

- Charles Schwab ("Creating a world of smarter investors.")

- Infinity ("It's not just a new car. It's all the best thinking.")

- Toyota Prius ("a car that sometimes runs on gas power and sometimes runs on electric power from a company that always runs on brainpower.")

- Adobe Systems ("...to bring ideas to life on the web, the printed page, and video.")

- Lean Cuisine ("Eat smart. Cook simple.")

Appealing to the Sage Consumer Archetype

The Sage consumer archetype loves learning for its own sake and is keenly interested in books, instructional videos, how-to advice, and the Internet. Products associated with intelligence, scientific or technological advancement, and engineering superiority are his greatest interest.

Even though the Sage, like all consumers, makes purchase decisions in his heart (or with his reptilian brain), the Sage has an extra special need to cloak his choices in rational armament.

So, when selling to the Sage consumer archetype, always provide numerous reasons that support a logical decision to buy. Emphasize benefits, benefits, benefits.

The Sage consumer thrives on feeling like an expert. Your sales promotion copy should never talk down to a Sage consumer.

Never underestimate a Sage consumer's intelligence or overestimate his knowledge. And always provide lots of supporting data.

The Take-Away: The Sage consumer desires products that reinforce his self-image as intelligent, knowledgeable and wise.

The Outlaw Archetype

The Outlaw archetype is variously known as the rebel, the rogue, the non-conformist, the outsider, the maverick, the wild man or woman, the iconoclast and the revolutionary.

Outlaws get their greatest gratification from being perceived as shocking, radical, outrageous, fearless and unconventional. The Outlaw thinks of himself as helping people by bending or breaking the rules.

At his best, the Outlaw sees himself as taking revenge, leading the revolution, and destroying what is not working (for himself or for society). At his worst, the Outlaw goes over to the dark side or becomes a criminal.

The Outlaw consumer may feel powerless, marginalized, trivialized or mistreated. She is often angry, disruptive or rebellious.

Products that appeal to Outlaw consumers help them feel free from the conventions of society.

If you want to heighten the anxiety of an Outlaw consumer, you can leverage her feeling powerless, angry, mistreated or under siege. Just be certain your product relieves those feelings and doesn't heighten them!

Outlaw Brands

- Harley-Davidson (motorcycles associated with outlaw biker clubs)

- Apple computers ("Think different.")

- The Gap (American clothing retailer tailors its stores "to appeal to unique markets" by developing multiple formats and designs)

- Calvin Klein (fashion apparel designer uses frequently controversial advertising campaigns)

- Robin Hood (mythical folklore hero known for robbing the rich to provide for the poor and fighting against injustice and tyranny)

- Zorro (fictional black-clad masked outlaw who defends the people of the land against tyrannical officials and other villains)

- Woodstock (1969 U.S. rock festival)

- Rebel Without a Cause

- On the Road

- Bonnie and Clyde

- Butch Cassidy and the Sundance Kid

- The Godfather

- Goodfellas

- Rolling Stone magazine

- tattoos, hippies, rappers

- MTV

- Fox TV

- Howard Stern (American radio host, humorist and media mogul dubbed a shock jock for his highly controversial use of scatological, sexual, and racial humor)

- Opium perfume (advertising campaign caused great controversy by showing a voluptuous model lying on her back wearing only a pair of stiletto heels)

- Captain Morgan rum ("Got a little Captain in you?")

- Milky Way Midnight, ("Dangerously bold chocolate.")

- Jack Daniels bourbon (Tennessee whiskey strongly linked to rock and roll, American biker culture, country music, and macho myths)

- Hathaway shirts (pirate-like eye patch on the man)

- The Scarlet Letter

- Huckleberry Finn

- Thelma and Louise

- Fried Green Tomatoes

- Madonna

- Jack Nicholson

- Darth Vader

- Wylie Coyote

Appealing to the Outlaw Consumer Archetype

The Outlaw consumer archetype identifies with products that are "edgy" or at odds with the mainstream values of society. This is readily apparent in the Outlaw's preferences in clothing fashion, jewelry, music, politics and entertainment.

The Outlaw consumer archetype is also attracted to products that literally destroy things, such as guns, or virtually, as many video games do.

Outlaw consumers are drawn to products that fly in the face of society's conventional ideas about health and safety, such as cigarettes, motorcycles, body piercing and tattoos.

Information products that appeal to the Outlaw consumer archetype generally provide advice on "beating the system," such as winning at craps or blackjack, retiring inexpensively overseas, unconventional or high-risk investing, etc.

The Take-Away: The Outlaw consumer archetype desires products that reinforce his self-image as a rebel, or that enable him to bend the rules of society, or that help him feel as though he is taking revenge against personal injustice.

The Ruler Archetype

The Ruler archetype is variously known as the boss, the manager, the leader, the aristocrat, the role model and the responsible citizen.

Rulers get their greatest gratification from being perceived as responsible, prosperous, and successful. The Ruler thinks of himself as helping people by exerting control.

Rulers enjoy organizing activities, setting policies, and making rules. Rulers like to think of themselves as being "in charge" and always in command of any situation.

The Ruler sees himself as being the noble, benevolent and successful leader of his family, group, organization or workplace. At his best, the Ruler desires to help the world. At his worst, the Ruler is an impatient, bossy, manipulative and authoritarian tyrant.

Famous Ruler Brands

- Winston Churchill

- Margaret Thatcher

- Any Supreme Court justice

- The Internal Revenue Service

- The White House

- IBM Corporation

- Brooks Brothers ("Generations of Style.")

- Microsoft

- American Express

- U.S. Forest Service ("Only you can prevent forest fires.")

- The Sharper Image ("For the person who has everything, we have everything else.")

- Hewlett-Packard

- Tylenol ("It's hospital recommended.")

- Intel

- Ralph Lauren

- Citibank

- Day-Timers

- Most HMOs, old-style banks, insurance companies and high-status law and investment firms.

- Home alarm systems

- Intercoms

- Zoned heating systems

- Automatic lawn-watering systems

Appealing to the Ruler Consumer Archetype

The Ruler consumer dislikes chaos and is attracted to products that create order and harmony, or that offer safety, technical assistance, protection, and predictability in a world of chaos.

Ruler consumers are particularly attracted to high-status products that enhance their self-image as powerful and successful. The typical trappings of the well-heeled Ruler consumer archetype are the Armani suit, the Rolex watch and the Mercedes-Benz automobile.

The Take-Away: The Ruler consumer archetype desires products that reinforce his image, status and prestige.

The Creator Archetype

The Creator archetype is variously known as the artist, the actor, the innovator, the inventor, the musician, the writer and the dreamer.

The Creator gets her major gratification by being perceived as creative, artistic and imaginative. She enjoys crafting something new, or creating something of enduring value, and collecting the accompanying plaudits.

The Creator consumer thinks of herself as innovative and self-expressive. She is inherently non-conformist and sees herself, not as fitting in to the commonplace, but as creating her own culture and expressing her own unique vision.

At her best, the Creator creates structures that influence culture and society. At her worst, the Creator is obsessed, self-absorbed, overly dramatic and a perfectionist.

Creator brands

- Georgia O'Keeffe
- Pablo Picasso
- Mozart
- Stephen Spielberg
- Do-it-yourself products
- Crayola crayons
- Martha Stewart

- Emeril Lagasse

- Williams-Sonoma

- Sherwin-Williams

- Singer sewing machines

- Home Depot ("You can do it. We can help.")

- Good Housekeeping

- House Beautiful

- B&B Italia furniture ("Timeless and treasured.")

- Bombay Sapphire gin ("Pour something priceless.")

- Sesame Street

- Kinko's ("Express yourself.")

Appealing to the Creator Consumer Archetype

The Creator consumer is driven to make something new and likes to work in places where creative projects take place - workshops, kitchens, gardens, studios, etc.

Creator consumers react well to products that are new, unique or unusual, and innovative, provided they reflect quality and imagination. Creator consumers are decidedly bored and intolerant of anything shoddy, mass-produced, unimaginative, or lacking in attention to detail.

Creator consumers are drawn to products that enable self-expression through options and choices. They love products that are artistically designed or encourage innovation.

When selling to the Creator consumer, always emphasize the do-it-yourself aspects of the product, or any feature that enables self-expression.

If you want to create anxiety in a Creator consumer, threaten her with a mediocre result, or worse - failure owing to poor execution. Then present your product or service as the solution to those undesirable outcomes.

The Take-Away: The Creator consumer archetype desires products that reinforce her image as creative, artistic and imaginative.

The Explorer Archetype

The Explorer archetype is variously known as the seeker, the adventurer, the iconoclast, the wanderer, the individualist, the pilgrim, the antihero and the rebel. He may feel restless, dissatisfied and bored.

Explorers get their greatest gratification from being perceived as seeking out new experiences, on a personal journey, escaping entrapment and boredom.

The Explorer likes to think of himself as experiencing a more authentic, fulfilling, unconventional life. He enjoys being free and discovering himself by exploring the world.

At his best, the Explorer sees himself as expressing his individuality and uniqueness. He is ambitious, autonomous, true to himself, and self-fulfilled.

At his worst, the Explorer is alienated, wandering aimlessly, and unable to fit in.

If you want to create anxiety in an Explorer consumer, make him feel he is getting trapped or giving in to conformity. Then offer your product or service as a relief for his fear of inner emptiness and non-being.

Explorer Brands

- Huckleberry Finn

- The Great Gatsby

- On the Road

- The Odyssey

- The Lone Ranger

- Star Trek ("To go boldly where no man has gone before.")

- Boats, snow mobiles, SUVs.

- U.S. Navy ("It's not a job. It's an adventure.")

- Ford Explorer ("No boundaries.")

- Hummer ("Like nothing else.")

- Jeep Wrangler ("Take your body where your mind has already wandered.")

- Goodyear tires ("Goodyear. We discover, you explore.")

- Individual sports: kayaking, biking, skiing, long distance running

- Explorer fashion: Levis, REI, Patagonia, Land's End.

- Burger King ("Have it your way.")

- Virgin Atlantic Airways

- Starbucks coffee (named for Ahab's adversary on the whale ship)

- Trex decks ("How far would you go if nothing was holding you back?")

- Amazon.com ("Earth's Biggest Selection.")

- Virginia Slims ("Find your own voice.")

- Goddard college ("Progressive education for creative minds.")

- Rockport ("Comfortable shoes for the journey.")

- Polo Sport ("Explorers, travelers and adventurers, since 1970.")

Appealing to the Explorer archetype

The Explorer consumer self-identifies with the individual vs. the group. Products and services that appeal to the Explorer consumer archetype help him express his individuality and feel free, non-conformist or pioneering (but not as much as the Outlaw consumer).

Explorer brand loyalty often emerges from products that are rugged, or used outdoors, or in dangerous or adventuresome activities. But because Explorer consumers seek out adventure, learning opportunities, and new experiences, they are equally good candidates for books and other information products that offer alternative occupations and lifestyles.

Explorer consumers have a wide range of interests and are motivated by their curiosity, passions and excitement. They can also be impulsive and prone to risk-taking.

Explorers are frequently dreamers ("Sell the dream!") but, owing to an insatiable desire for stimulation, they can lack focus and attention to detail.

The Take-Away: The Explorer consumer archetype desires products that reinforce his image as an individual, adventurer, and nonconformist.

The Magician Archetype

The Magician archetype is variously known as the visionary, the catalyst, the innovator, the inventor, the charismatic leader, the shaman, the healer, and the medicine man or woman.

Magicians get their greatest gratification from being perceived as capable of making dreams come true.

Magicians think of themselves as mystical, as understanding how the world works, as being visionaries, and as having transformative abilities.

The Magician often sees herself as a miracle worker, as experiencing the "flow," and as creating magical or transformative moments. She enjoys and indulges hunches and extrasensory or synchronistic experiences.

The Magician may feel she has a gift for creating win-win outcomes. At her best, the Magician is able to move from visionary to manifestation. At her worst, she is manipulative or practices the occult.

If you want to create anxiety in a Magician, play on her fear of unanticipated negative consequences - and offer her your product or service as the antidote.

Magician Brands

- Harry Potter

- Mary Poppins

- Field of Dreams

- Like Water for Chocolate

- Jim Collins' book ("From Good to Great.")

- Apple's iPod

- Sparkling water

- Champagne

- Smirnoff gin ("Clearly original.")

- General Foods International Coffees

- Calgon ("Take me away.")

- Spas

- Rainbows, shooting stars, flying saucers

- Cruise lines

- Virtually all New Age products

- Mind-body medicine

- New Balance ("Turn off your computer. Turn off your fax machine. Turn off your cell phone. Connect with yourself.")

- Ajax cleanser ("The White Knight.")

- Energizer bunny ("He keeps going and going and ...")

- MasterCard ("...priceless. For everything else, there's MasterCard")

- Digital cameras

- Oil of Olay ("Share the secret of a younger looking you.")

- Perrier ("The champagne of mineral water.")

- Xerox copiers

- DuPont ("The miracles of science.")

- Bristol-Myers Squibb ("Hope, triumph, and the miracle of medicine.")

- Yellow Pages ("Let your fingers do the walking.")

- Rolex, ("An obsession with perfection.")

- Weight Watchers ("Stop Dieting - Start Living.")

Appealing to the Magician Consumer Archetype

Magician consumers are right-brained and intuitive. They are frequently charismatic business leaders, successful politicians, and influential marketers who excel at understanding human behavior. Often Magician consumers are athletes and entrepreneurs.

The Magician consumer is generally an agent of change. She is inner-directed and more likely to look within herself for answers vs. being influenced by others.

That means selling to the Magician consumer requires a light touch; she does not like to feel manipulated. The Magician consumer must come to her own conclusions about whether your product or service is appropriate for her.

The Take-Away: The Magician consumer archetype desires products that confirm her self-image as an innovator, inventor and transformer.

The Innocent Archetype

The Innocent Archetype is variously known as the traditionalist, the mystic, the saint, the romantic and the dreamer.

The Innocent gets her greatest gratification from being perceived as doing things "right." She is honest, näive, forgiving, trusting, optimistic and utopian.

The Innocent thinks of herself as moral, law-abiding and exemplifying integrity. She sees herself as an advocate for peace, simplicity and conformity to nature. Sometimes, she imagines herself as having an almost mystical sense of oneness.

The Innocent aspires to be happy - even to experience paradise. She may be overly dependent - too trusting and even subservient to authority. Generally, she is serene, calm and peaceful.

The Innocent wants life to be easy. At her best, the Innocent displays spontaneity, faith, purity and optimism. At her worst, she is repressed and mired in denial about life's harsher realities.

If you want to induce anxiety in an Innocent consumer, exploit her fear of doing something wrong or bad that will result in unpleasantness or punishment. Then offer your product or service as the solution that guarantees peace and harmony.

Innocent Brands

- Chicken Soup for the Soul

- All I Really Need to Know I Learned in Kindergarten

- Doris Day

- Meg Ryan

- Tom Hanks

- Forest Gump

- The PBS network

- Keds

- Disney

- Ronald McDonald

- McDonald's

- Baskin-Robbins ("31 flavors")

- Pillsbury Doughboy

- Ivory soap ("99 44/100 percent pure .... and it FLOATS!")

- Cotton ("the fabric of our lives")

- Whole and organic foods

- Doubletree Hotels ("the perfect getaway")

- Clairol Herbal Essence shampoo ("a totally organic

experience with style")

- Real Simple magazine ("Do less, have more.")

- Belvedere vodka ("The same way my father made it. The same way his father made it.")

- Maxwell House ("Make every day good to the last drop.")

- Michelin tires ("Because so much is riding on your tires," featuring babies and implying safety)

- IKEA (Means "common sense.")

- Coke ("It's the real thing" and "I'd like to build the world a home and furnish it with love...")

- The Amish

- All things New Age ("utopian spiritual movement")

Appealing to the Innocent Consumer Archetype

The Innocent consumer is attracted to products associated with goodness, morality, simplicity, nostalgia and childhood.

Honesty, cleanliness, wholesomeness, and health are highly valued criteria for the Innocent consumer archetype, and she is attracted to products that reflect these qualities.

Be extra vigilant in projecting honesty and integrity in your communications to Innocent consumers. They value candor and integrity, and are turned off by hype, so keep you sales promotion messages simple and straight-forward.

The Take-Away: The Innocent consumer archetype desires products that reinforce her self-image as virtuous, serene and in harmony with the world.

The Jester Archetype

The Jester archetype is variously known as the fool, the trickster, the joker, the clown, the entertainer and the comedian.

The Jester gets his greatest gratification from being perceived as always having a fun time and as lightening up the world for others. He thinks of himself as bringing joy to others by playing, making jokes and being funny.

The Jester may suffer from boredom, never taking anything seriously, and seeing life as a big game. Believing that other, more serious types are in charge, he responds by living "one day at a time" and experiencing life "in the moment."

The typical Jester is extraordinarily clever, capable of innovative, out-of-the-box thinking. But sometimes he is too smart for his own good and willing to break the rules to point out or deal with the absurdities of modern life.

At his best, the Jester brings joy to others. But sometimes the Jester uses his cleverness to trick others, to get out of trouble, or to circumvent obstacles and responsibility. At his worst, the Jester is self-indulgent, irresponsible, engaging in mean-spirited pranks, or frittering away his life.

Jester Brands

- Bugs Bunny

- Will Rogers

- John Stewart

- Buster Keaton

- Charlie Chaplin

- Barbra Streisand in What's Up, Doc?

- Rene Zellweger in Nurse Betty

- Woody Allen in Zelig

- Milk ("Got Milk?" with celebrities sporting milk mustaches)

- Snickers candy bar (a form of laughter)

- Snack foods - Pringles ("Everything Pops with Pringles.")

- Liquor - Parrot Bay; Kahlua ("Anything goes.")

- Alka-Seltzer ("Mamma Mia, that's a spicy meatball.")

- Joe Camel (advertising mascot for Camel cigarettes)

- Pepsi ("Be Young, Have Fun, Drink Pepsi.")

- Southwest Airlines ("[Ding.] You are now free to move about the country.")

- Starkist tuna ("Sorry, Charlie. Starkist wants tuna that tastes good, not tuna with good taste.")

- Miller Lite (think Dick Butkus and Bubba Smith)

- Teva sandals ("Make your feet feel like a kid again.")

- Yahoo! ("Do you Yahoo?")

- Hyundai Elantra ("Driving is believing.")

- MetLife (ads featuring Peanuts characters)

- Butterfingers (commercials featuring Bart Simpson)

- Trix cereal ("Silly rabbit, Trix are for kids.")

Appealing to the Jester Consumer Archetype

Jester consumers want products that are intrinsically fun, or that enable people to have a good time.

The Jester consumer is attracted to products sold by companies that appear to be fun-loving and free-wheeling (Yahoo!; The Motley Fools). Additionally, the Jester consumer prefers products that are differentiated from self-important, overconfident or "stuffy" brands e.g. MetLife (blimp) vs. Prudential (Rock of Gibraltar).

If the Jester consumer is insecure - and many are - he will be attracted to products that enable him to fit in or feel as though he belongs.

If you want to take the Jester out of his comfort zone, try forcing him to be serious - even overly serious - where he can't escape to merriment and mirth.

The Take-Away: The Jester consumer archetype just wants to have fun and is attracted to products that enable people to have a good time.

The Caregiver Archetype

The Caregiver archetype is variously known as the caretaker, the parent, the saint, the helper and the supporter.

The Caregiver gets her greatest gratification from being perceived as always doing things for others. She thinks of herself as altruistic, caring, nurturing and generous.

The Caregiver sees herself as concerned for the larger world and as demonstrated by performing her role of protecting others from harm. She enjoys caring for and nurturing her dependents, balancing her own needs with concern for, and attending to the needs of others who are less capable.

The Caregiver loathes selfishness and ingratitude. She may feel underappreciated, which frustrates and angers her. She fears being perceived as a loser just because she cares for others.

At her best, the Caregiver is compassionate and generous. At her worst, the Caregiver is capable of trying to give her dependents a guilt trip, or of being an enabler who allows loved ones to behave in ways that are destructive. At her extreme worst, the Caregiver is a martyr.

Caregiver Brands

- Nurses, teachers, neighborhood cop, old-fashioned country doctor

- Princess Diana (noted for her sense of compassion and high-profile charity work)

- Mother Teresa (ministered to the poor, sick, orphaned, and dying)

- Mister Rogers ("I like you just the way you are. You know that, don't you?")

- Albert Schweitzer (humanitarian and Nobel Peace Prize winner for his philosophy of "reverence for life")

- Ronald Reagan (His ability to connect with the American people earned him the laudatory moniker, "The Great Communicator.")

- Walter Cronkite ("the most trusted man in America"; also a Sage)

- Blue Cross/Blue Shield (community-based healthcare coverage companies)

- Marcus Welby, M.D. (a family practitioner with a kind bedside manner)

- "Parents: the antidrug."

- AT&T ("Reach out and touch someone.")

- Campbell's soup ("Um, um...Good!")

- Land's End (famous for its "Guaranteed. Period." policy, which allows for returns or exchanges at any time and for any reason.)

- Band-Aid adhesive bandages ("Heals the wound fast, heals the hurt faster.")

- Dr. Scholl's brand of foot care products

- Norman Rockwell (famous for illustrations of everyday life scenarios)

- Stouffer's ("Nothing comes closer to home.")

- Sunsweet ("To your health.")

- Sallie Mae, BankOne, First Union, Bank of America

- Rogaine ("Your dad wants you to have things he never had. Like hair.")

- GE ("We bring good things to life.")

- The Salvation Army (serves the poor, destitute and hungry by meeting both their physical and spiritual needs)

- United Way (a coalition of charitable organizations in the United States)

- Habitat for Humanity (non-profit organization devoted to building "simple, decent, and affordable" housing using volunteer labor)

- Nordstrom ("Our number one goal is to provide outstanding customer service.")

- Volvo (Founder vowed to produce the safest cars possible.)

- Wheaties ("The breakfast of champions")

Appealing to the Caregiver Consumer Archetype

The Caregiver consumer archetype is alive and thriving in people who attend to maintaining other people or things, or who feel concern or interest in conserving, sustaining or repairing the physical world. Caregiver consumers are often occupied with cleaning and mending clothes and homes; gardening; caring for the sick and the elderly.

Everyone wants to be loved and nurtured, and no one more so than the Caregiver, whose major gratification is derived from helping others. Not surprisingly, Caregiver consumers are drawn to businesses that provide exceptional customer service.

Caregiver consumers gravitate to products that provide support for families such as fast food restaurants, minivans, family recreation and vacation destinations, etc. Products that are associated with nurturance such as comfort foods (cookies, milk, soup, etc.) are usually Caregiver brands.

Additional brands that appeal to the Caregiver consumer include anything related to health and education, or helping others (including politics, non-profit causes and charitable activities), or that enable people to care for themselves.

Your sales letter can appeal to Caregiver consumers by depicting someone in need, then offering a product or service that rescues or comforts.

Of utmost importance is that your sales promotion copy is empathetic. Story-telling that features caring, communication (especially listening), integrity and trust strike a responsive chord in the Caregiver consumer and will produce the best response.

The Take-Away: The Caregiver consumer archetype desires products that reinforce her self-image as caring for others or protecting them from harm.

The Lover Archetype

The Lover archetype is variously known as the partner, the friend, the intimate, the matchmaker, the enthusiast, the connoisseur, the sensualist, the spouse, the team builder and the harmonizer.

The Lover gets her greatest gratification from being in a relationship with other people, her work, her experiences and the surroundings she loves. Typically the Lover seeks great sex or a great romance.

The Lover thinks of herself as being physically, emotionally, and in every other way attractive and desirable.

The Lover sees herself as being passionate, seductive and committed. She enjoys seeking and attaining intimacy and experiencing sensual pleasure.

The Lover may feel alone, unwanted and unloved. If so, she will do anything and everything to attract and please others.

And her best, the Lover will experience spiritual love, self-acceptance and ecstasy. At her worst, the Lover will experience promiscuity, obsession, jealousy and envy.

Lover Brands

Lover brands are common in the cosmetics, jewelry, fashion and travel industries.

- Hallmark cards ("When you care enough to send the very best")

- Chanel No. 5 fragrance ("A woman should wear

fragrance wherever she expects to be kissed.")

- Revlon ("Feel like a woman.")

- Calvin Klein's Obsession ("Between love and madness lies Obsession.")

- Victoria's Secret

- Kay Jewelers ("Every kiss begins with Kay.")

- Godiva chocolate

- Barilla pasta ("To eat doesn't mean only to feed yourself - it means also to love yourself.")

- Gevalia Kaffe ("Making coffee lovers smile since 1853")

- Jordache jeans

- Häagen Dazs ice cream ("Made like no other.")

- Virginia Tourism Commission ("Virginia is for lovers.")

- Clark Gable, Cary Grant, Sophia Loren, Elizabeth Taylor

- Titanic

- Casablanca

- Hennessy Cognac ("Hennessy. Mix accordingly.")

- Concord gold diamond watch ("Style defined")

- Caress moisturizing bath products ("Before you dress, Caress.")

- Absolut vodka ("Absolut magic.")

- Jaguar automobiles ("Don't dream it. Drive it!")

Appealing to the Lover Consumer Archetype

The Lover consumer archetype wants more than anything else to feel loved. She thinks of herself as beautiful (or handsome) and special. She wants to attract, give love, and express affection in intimate and pleasurable ways.

The Lover consumer wants a deeper connection that is intimate, genuine, personal and sensual. She likes being singled out for attention and needs to feel special, cared for and nurtured.

The Take-Away: The Lover consumer archetype prefers products that are one of a kind, unusual, or tailored especially for her. She requires quality, not for status, but for the enhanced pleasure it represents.

The Regular Guy/Regular Gal Archetype

The Regular Guy/Gal archetype is variously known as the good old boy, the regular Jane, Everyman, the common man, the guy or gal next door, the realist, the working stiff, the solid citizen and the good neighbor.

The Regular Guy gets his greatest gratification from connecting with other people. He fears standing out, seeming to put on airs, and being exiled or rejected as a result.

The Regular Guy thinks of himself as genuine, realistic, unpretentious, down-to-earth, possessing ordinary solid virtues and displaying the common touch. He enjoys belonging to and blending in with the group, both offering and accepting help and friendship.

The Regular Guy fears feeling abandoned and alone, or being alienated from others. At his worst he is willing to be abused rather than be alone, or to be a part of a lynch-mob, willing to go along with abuse in order to be one of the gang.

At his best, the Regular Guy is an empathetic humanitarian who believes in the natural dignity of every person, regardless of his or her abilities or circumstances.

The Regular Guy/Regular Gal consumer archetype is unfailingly frugal, whether or not he or she has money.

Regular Guy/Gal Brands

- Country-Western music
- Tomb of the Unknown Soldier

- All in the Family

- Cheers, (where everybody knows your name)

- Roseanne

- Ally McBeal (just as neurotic as anyone else)

- Beer (vs. wine)

- Hockey (vs. tennis or golf)

- Glenlivet whisky ("In some places, athletes are revered as gods. This is not one of those places. One place, one whisky.")

- Jim Beam ("Real friends. Real bourbon.")

- Perdue chicken ("It takes a tough man to make a tender chicken.")

- Snapple ("Made from the best stuff on Earth.")

- Wendy's

- Paul Newman

- Wrangler jeans ("There's a bit of the West in all of us.")

- The Myers-Briggs Type Indicator (the people's psychological tool)

- VISA vs. American Express

- MetLife ("Have you met life today? Get Met. It pays.")

- GEICO ("Save a lot of money on your car insurance.")

- Avis ("We try harder.")

- Unions vs. management

- Ben & Jerry's (Over one million free cones are given away each year, prompting the company's ad slogan, "Be One in a Million.")

The Take-Away: The Regular Guy/Regular Gal consumer archetype is drawn to products that have a down-home, no-nonsense quality to them.

The value of archetypes to the copywriter

The collective unconscious, according to Jung, manifested itself in the form of primordial images or archetypes that showed up in dreams, art, religion, legends, fairy tales, mythology, etc. By symbolizing our core human desires, archetypes can evoke strong, deep emotions.

But the emotional connection between your product or brand and the unconscious motivations of prospective customers can not be adequately understood through quantitative modes of research. So don't ask me for proof. There is only anecdotal evidence. The basic idea is that strong archetypal features will resonate with your target audience.

"The goal isn't to explain the origins of these often irrational needs, but to realize that they are there," says marketing consultant Seth Godin. "Gravity's causes are unknown, but we still need to factor it in to our lives. Same with archetypes. We don't have to understand them to leverage them."

There are other models that identify many more than these 12 archetypes. Your brand may be represented by more than one archetype, and your prospective customers are usually represented by more than one consumer archetype.

Clint Eastwood, in his early Western movies, represents both an Outlaw archetype and a Hero archetype. Dorothy in the Wizard of Oz is both an Innocent and an Explorer. Luke Skywalker from the Star Wars movies is both a Hero and an Explorer. Yoda is both a Sage and a Magician.

Similarly, blue jeans can appeal to the Regular Guy/Regular

Gal as well as the Outlaw and the Explorer. Perfume can be positioned for both the Lover and the Magician. Most dedicated homemakers are both Creators and Caregivers.

Investment advice can be branded to appeal to both the Ruler and the Sage. In fact, the Sage consumer archetype is fundamentally a target for all information products because the Sage has an almost insatiable desire for information.

Any product whose primary benefit or feature is performance, whether it be an automobile, a copier, or a wrist watch, can be positioned to appeal to the Hero. In fact, Gerber believes all men fantasize about being the Hero and suggests appealing to the Hero consumer archetype is the easiest and most appropriate strategy for most products that are designed for men.

Similarly, Gerber believes all women fantasize about being wives and homemakers, and any almost any product can be sold to women by positioning it to appeal to their desire to be more attractive to men. This is not exactly The Feminine Mystique or politically correct, but it does have its roots in the collective unconscious. I think most people unconsciously find the archetype that serves them best. Decide for yourself.

I recommend using the consumer archetype model to begin a copywriting or marketing assignment because it helps bring your targeted customer into focus. Using archetypes to create characters and write emotional stories about your product is today's most effective strategy for connecting with buyers.

About Peter A. Schaible

Peter creates keyword-rich, search-engine-optimized, rapid conversation landing pages, sales letter landing pages, and other written components of websites and direct response marketing campaigns.

"If your website can't be found by Google, or isn't ranked highly in Google search results, it virtually doesn't exist," he says.

An experienced direct response advertising copywriter prior to the Internet, Peter was an early convert to the research pioneered by Don Nicholas and his discovery of the Mequoda System.

He has extensive experience in marketing communications, including as an editor of newsletters for the National Exchange Carrier Association (a U.S. telecommunications industry association), AT&T and IBM Corporation.

For more than 20 years he has been president of SunDance New Media, his own marketing communications consulting firm.

Before launching SunDance, he was director of communications for the United States Golf Association, where he supervised the publication of two magazines and managed the press tent at the U.S. Open and other national golf championships.

You can find Peter's contact information at his company website, www.sdnm.com.